Under the of the Milky Way Galaxy

Wisconsin Poems

Under the Tail
of the Milky Way
Galaxy

by Ethel Mortenson Davis

Author of:

I Sleep Between the Moons of New Mexico, 2010
White Ermine Across Her Shoulders, 2011
The Healer, 2016
Here We Breathe in Sky and Out Sky, 2016

*All of Ethel Mortenson Davis's books can be ordered from the
gallery at https://www.galleriacarnaval.com, 4018 Ice Caves Road,
NM 53, Mile Marker 46, El Morro, NM 87321*

Dedication

To Sonja and Mary, Sophia, Phoebe, William, and Joey with love

Acknowledgments

"A Day," *Indra's Net.* 2017. United Kingdom: Bennison Books, p. 41.

"An Evening," *Wisconsin Poets' Calendar 2017*, Barnard, Francha and Lauter, Estella, ed. 2016. Eau Claire, WI: Wisconsin Fellowship of Poets, p. 66.

"Escape," *An Ariel Anthology.* December 2015.

"Cold," *Poetry Breakfast.* December 4, 2017, accessed at https://poetrybreakfast.com/2017/12/04/cold-a-poem-by-ethel-mortenson-davis. Washburn, WI: Ariel Woods Books, p. 64.

"Laborer," *Blue Heron Review*, issue 7, Winter 2017, accessed at https://blueheronreview.com/blue-heron-review-issue-7-winter-2017.

"Night Ride," *Bramble*, Summer 2018, David Southward, ed. Wisconsin Fellowship of Poets, p. 32.

"Wings," *Blue Heron Review*, issue 9, Winter 2018, accessed at https://blueheronreview.com/blue-heron-review-issue-9-winter-2018.

"Winter Solstice," *Poetry Breakfast.* December 21, 2017, accessed at https://poetrybreakfast.com/2017/12/21/winter-solstice-a-poem-by-ethel-mortenson-davis

Table of Contents

Presentation

The young father
bound
his newborn daughter
across his chest
and then slipped on his skis.

This was a cold February
in the land of lakes and trees
with dancing green lights.

Here he connected,
just as his ancestors
before him connected,
to the starry night,

just as his daughter
will someday bind
her infant
across her heart,
presenting a new life
under the milky-green
foam of stars,

under the great tail
of the Milky Way Galaxy
above her shoulders.

Cold

Fresh snow
with the same fox trail
ahead of us
each morning.

The cold at times
becomes unmovable,
but we must
meet her at her throat;

we must reach down
inside ourselves
for strength,
or we will be swallowed up

like the coyote
that morning
who stood his ground,
unmovable,

his yellow eyes
shadowing our eyes.

New Gables

There are many times
when our houses
fall down around us,
when no part is left
recognizable.

Then we must pick
the best of the old stones
to build new rooms.

But we must also take
new maple,
just sawn,
white like the sands
along Lake Michigan,
and build something shining.

We must make brand new gables
whose attic windows
are left open for birds
to fly through,
the birds of heaven,

the barn owl
who finds shelter
for her life.

Cricket

Tonight, black cricket,
    if you sing your golden song,
you can have my room.

Restoration

The lips of the rain,
soft at first,
become
cold and stiff
from last night's
freezing temperatures.

Out on the lake
the black-winged pelicans
fish in huddles.
They are restored
to their ancient places,
the Great Lakes.

If only we could restore
the people to their rightful places,
bringing young and old back
to their ancient lands.

Instead millions are pushed out
from wars and famines
into a great movement

like schools of fish,
swarming,
moving like a great wheel
across the face of the deep.

Forgiveness

Before you come
into the wilderness
you must leave
your anger and hate
behind you.

You must open your heart
and extend your arms

before you can see
the new groundcover plants
whose leaves feel
like a baby's skin.

Look!
A yellow swallowtail.

She is leading us
through the shaded trees
and wants us to follow.

Wings

There is a part
of me
that walks and talks and sees,
but then there is
another one
that has parts of wings:

wings that take me
to the highest green cliff,
then drops me to the sea
to catch a ride on the back
of the dragonfly
as he crosses the land —

wings
that take me
to the farthest planet,
the red one,

then pulls me
back to the forest
where green moss
clings to the north side
of trees
in winter's cascade
of blue shadows on snow
and sparkling sun.

Wrinkled Skin

This morning
the trunks of cedar trees
felt skin-like,
looking like wrinkled
elephant skin —

elephants cornered
throughout Africa,
poached, killed
for money.

One man spent most
of his life protecting them.

When he died recently,
the elephants walked
in single-file to his house
where he lay in state,
circling his house and
staying for some time.

Animals and birds know
when people want to
protect them,

show grace and gratitude.
They wait for us to save them,

the animals,
the cedars,
the wrinkled skin.

Wooly Bear Caterpillar

I've come to lay
my head again in your lap
this wooly bear morning:
frost in the air,
the sky unbelievably blue,
the leaves red-orange.

I reach down and touch
the softness of the caterpillar's
black and brown bands.
She quickly springs into a ball —
so strong, so resilient:

strong enough to survive
90 below zero in arctic winters,
spinning a cocoon
and then in spring
turning into a Golden Isabella moth.

This strength is something
to take home with us,
to rid us of our toxic relationships,
disregarding them like clothing
we let drop around our ankles
and step away from
with a new nakedness,
frankness,

ready to start building
new cocoons that turn us
into golden moths.

Door

There,
in the bright morning,
Hepatica,
whose leaves stay alive
under the dead layer
all winter,
send up flowers
before all others.

It is here where
the pale pink and lavender
are the door opening
to where my god lives:

her angels are the birds
opening their wings.

Flight

Was it the spring stream,
flowing out of the escarpment,
tumbling, bubbling over fallen birch trees?

Or was it the large, sloppy snowflakes
falling in the spring morning's forest,
as trees held their breath,
held their breathing
for the sun to overtake the cold,

that made my wings open and close,

readying me to take flight?

Fractals

Wilderness embraces us
this wet morning
with pictures of chaos:

fractals,
repeating patterns
of symmetry
that quiets,
sets our minds free.

These lovely patterns
in trees, rivers, coastlines,
mountains, and seashells
give us designs that are lovely . . .

like the wild dogwood,
a signature tree in the forest,
whose fractal symmetry
is like no other.

The most beautiful grace
I have ever seen
brings rest to our minds,
our souls.

Heaven

An astronaut that repaired
the Hubble spacecraft
said recently
that when he stepped out
on his first spacewalk
and saw the lighted
blue and white earth
underneath him,

he knew
he was looking
at heaven.

I wonder how
we would have thought
of the land, the animals,
and the people
if we would have known
our earth was heaven?

If this was all the heaven
there will ever be?

Laborer

He was dressed
like a laborer
bending around in the yard
in working clothes.
He whistled tunes
that were classical symphonies.

I thought, how strange
he is dressed —
yet knows these tunes.
He should be dressed
in a beautiful coat like Joseph's.

I went to the window,
looking for him,
still hearing his whistling,
but then realized
I was waking from a dream —

like the Navajo holy woman
chanting under my window
that early morning.

I went to all the windows
to catch a glimpse of her,
but then realized
she was part of my dream.

Who are these people?

I think they are the healers
that repair
the holes in the universe,
the tear,
the rift just outside my window.

Ladies Need Fur Coats

She went to the great black first,
then the bay.

She had carrots
in one of her coat pockets.

"Which pocket?" She asked.

Their soft muzzles always
found the right one,
happy to munch the carrots.

Then one day
the black was gone,
his stall cleaned out,
and shovels put in his place.

"Where's Dick?" she asked.

"He went to the fox farm because
ladies need fur coats," he said.

The bay remained
for a number of years,
sleeping in the winter sun
with his head too low to the ground.

Then one day the bay too
was gone,
his great body and his work
folded into the fields
outside his window.

Lotus

The water lotus
      should not be so beautiful
      in this war-torn world.

Northwest Cedars

The trees whisper.

He will not lay us low
with the blade,
or render us invisible
with the axe —

so we will light his way
with birds,
music to titillate
his broken heart.

We will get the white bear
to lay salmon at our feet,
streams overflowing
with the red fish.

He believes
he is kin to us
as he climbs
the rocky cliffs
and looks out
across the valley,
exchanging chemicals
with us

like human beings
exchanging pheromones.

The Builder

We were hoping
to catch a glimpse of
the one who made this place,
a summer place
by the water.

We wanted to see him or her,
but we kept missing him.

Perhaps if we rise
early in the morning
when it is still dark
we will glimpse this one.

Or if we delay in the evening,
when the summer light
lays on our shoulders
for endless hours,
we will see the builder.

I know he or she has left gifts everywhere,
like the pile of stones
at the water's edge.

It is a masterful display
of color and size,
each one shiny
from the motion of water,

a universe within itself.

The Cloak

The earth dresses in
    the cloak of humanity,
but it does not fit.

Trees

The trees have always
extended their hands to us,
making deep, cool chambers
of cedar, birch and maple
where enlightenment is possible.

But we, in turn,
have responded
with a sharp slap
to the side of their face.

The women of Kenya
started a green revolution
across their land:
women planting trees
in hope of stopping
the encroaching desert,

trees that created a moist climate,
pulling water to the parched lips of Kenya.

When our great, great, grandchildren
ask us what we have done
to save the trees on our planet,
will we be the generation of enlightenment,
or one with empty hands?

Wilderness

For Brand Windmiller

You take a boy,
ten or eleven,
and put him
into the wilderness,

let him do
the hard work
of canoeing
before the destructive
influences permeate him,

and
let the wilderness
finish his training.

Let him eat berries and nuts,
and let him hear the sound of
the red-eyed loon
as she carries her young
on her back.

If once is not enough,
bring him again.
Let the wilderness
do her work.

Early in the morning
push the bow
into the darkness
as the white fog
sits on top the water.

Aware

One doesn't unravel
when branches strain
with too much snow,
or the cold
makes the ground
sound hollow —
an empty sound.

One doesn't unravel,
but instead the cold
wakes us up —
sharpens us
like the jagged ice
along the bay,

crying out to us,
"Stay back"
"Stay aware!"

Better Place

Perhaps,
if we didn't want
to go to a better place —
they said when he died
he went to a better place —
we would want to take care
of the earth
and other species.

Perhaps,
if we thought
of the earth
as our better place,
we would revere it —
the forest and animals
would be our cathedral.

This morning
the cornered possum
lay down and played dead
until the children and dog left.
Then she got up and ran away,

returning to her cherished life,
her better place.

Discovery

It is because
the earth is tilted
this time of year,
the sun brightest at sunrise,
October light exceptional,

that I can see
silver threads strung
across my path
along the ancient forest floor,

thousands of gleaming strings
made by tree snails or slugs,
trails of lubricant
caught by sunlight
in a mathematical moment:

glistening chains we put
around our necks
to take home with us
to put in our favorite drawer —
the one labeled "DISCOVERIES"—
there in the back of our mind.

Fawn

The rain yields
to the drying wind,
trilliums ceasing,
forget-me-nots thriving,

the dogs loving
the walk in the morning rain.

The afternoon sun
puts the old dog to sleep.

Tomorrow
the flickering light
will lock
the fawn in hiding
in the meadow grasses
in the deep forest.

Fellow Travelers

The older Oriental woman
was not nice.
The younger men
of European descent
accompanied him.
Actually, they never
left his side.

He thought if he
went far enough away
they would go away,
but they did not.

Even when he was dying
they frightened him.
That was why he moved
far away — to New York.
Perhaps all his problems
would go away.
But they did not.

He told us this at the last.
He didn't want to hurt us.

When you were little
the voices in your head
were telling you things.

I made a mental note,

"Something is wrong."

Forest

It's where the snow lies
inside the beating heart;
the forest,
who speaks in voices
across the wind,
waiting for the conductor
to begin
its movement spring-ward:

where teeth tear open
the flesh of a kill,
wolfing it down in mouthfuls
before another comes
to claim it as its own —

where mankind
has nailed her hindquarters
to a board.

In her anguish
and suffering
the forest
still presents us
with gifts
indescribable.

Goldfinch

A small goldfinch
hit our glass door.
He lay unconscious —
in the process of dying.

"I will return later
when he is gone,"
she said.
"He needs quiet
and stillness."

When she checked again
the bird was sitting up
and awake.
Life had come back to him.

"He will be stronger
and cherish life more,"
she thought.
"A bright spot
in his spring world,"

like the green
moss-covered stone
this winter —
shining out from under
the deep winter snows.

When she returned
he was gone.

Juno

Nearly every night
Juno wakes me
with eerie sounds,

sounds that are crying,
tormented
from deep dreams.

She came to our gate
eleven years ago, starving,
having recently had puppies.

After feeding her for days,
she never tried to go back
to them,

so I thought they were dead
or taken from her.

I go to her in the night,
comforting her,
telling her she is now safe,

telling her
humans are both tormentors
and saviors.

Kinship

I've come again
to watch your woods,
snow up to my thighs,
winds flying
across the tops of trees —
like when I was little.

On windy days
I would run
into the woods
and listen to the wind
roaring across the tops
of trees,

but stillness would
be beneath.

I think of trees
as family,
kin.

Lesser World

I saw them in strings,
making the shape of V's,

Canadian geese
flying high enough
to use the lake's edge
as their guide:
blue-green water
with white foam
at the edges,
over rushes with dark red plumes
on their trek
southward.

For our world will
become lesser
without them,
not as full of life
as the wet summer
has been

while we wait
for the silent season
of winter —

and for the quiet winter
of our life.

Liberation

An old man leaves
a federal prison,
free at last.
He has spent
most of his life
behind bars
for a crime
he did not commit.

The air is as sweet
as any he has known.
He steps into freedom.

This morning
a white butterfly,
with black accents
I could not identify,
was caught in a spider's web.

I pulled him from
his bondage.
He was still alive
and eager to fly.

He flew into the forest
rich with oxygen,
a freedom he had thought
would never again be his.

And there in the sundrenched trees
he became giddy
on pulsing, cooling waves of air.

Lost

This morning,
when we saw a cedar forest
whose trees seemed
as if they were from another world,

we saw a child's tale —
witches and goblins hiding
behind every tree trunk
on the soft fallen cedar floors.

Since we have moved
to this land of lakes and forests,
my body has moved,
but not my spirit.

It is still circling,
soaring in the sky,
keeping from lighting,
not sure whether
it will land

like the sandhill crane
this morning
circling the shores
of Lake Michigan,
not lighting,
appearing to be lost.

Newport Beach

It is the end
of Door Peninsula,
the Newport Beach forest,

less dense now
from the gale winds
of last September
that toppled dead trees,
crisscrossing their trunks
ahead on our path
amidst living, smaller trees.

Morning fog drips
on the top of our heads and faces
from its skyscraper canopy.

Night Ride

Come with me,
down to where the trees are,
for there is a line of sky
without clouds,
and soon the earth
will be the color of red honey.

Come with me,
for there is enough feed
for the horses,
and when we stop to sleep
we'll keep the dogs close
to warm us.

Come with me,
for the songs of the Ancients
are calling.
Orion is straight above our heads,
and we must make
this night's journey.

Open Water

Today we saw
black cormorants flying
close to the icy shore,

looking for open water.

We too look for open water
in our lives,
places that will
nourish and sustain us,

propel us through rocks and ice
that entangle us,
grab at our limbs
and minds, and bury us.

We yearn
for the boundless waters
of this vast lake

as glistening
black cormorants
yearn for spring's
warming light.

Player

When I awake
I will not go to the theater,
play parts, do different characters,
but will be who I am.

I will never go back
to that again,
but will go where
there is wilderness and wildlife,
running water, and laps of waves.

See, snorting deer,

I am my raw self.
I have no rifle,
and my bent toward you
is harmony.

Poems

The universe
throws out poems
across the stars,

but only the poet
catches them.

Reach

Her reach finds
small openings
in the forest canopy
until the carpet
at the bottom brings
every kind of plant and fern to formation.

These are true families
that enjoy each other's company —
some living at the top of hills,
other kinds in depressions —
trees that are dependent
on plants around them,
plants that only live by certain trees.

Step lightly.
Speak in whispers,
for there are newborns sleeping
everywhere.

Snow-Laden Woods

The snow-laden woods
are like the earth
starting over.

We, too,
are starting over
each day —
with renewed eyes
that look beyond the bay
and into the stars.

Branches of trees
on both sides of us
are intertwined across the path.

An Anishinaabe woman
once said to me,

"The trees are holding hands."

Sisters as Flowers

I think of one as a rose,
feminine yet voluptuous,
a powerful scent,
delicate like no other,
the first flower you go to
in the garden —

the oldest as a lily,
singular and strong,
standing apart from all the rest,
an example to all her sisters —

and then the white daisy,
clean and fresh
and wholly authentic—
one to have in your corner.

The Art of Craig Blietz

1

His art is of cows, goats, and pigs,
but mainly dairy cows, Holsteins,

great portraits of black and white Holsteins
posing with dignity and grace,
one with a large, bulging vein
running the length of the under belly
to its udder,

portraits rich in painterly quality,
showing a wondrous love for these animals.

2

A downed cow,
too sick to get on its feet,
is dragged with chains
to the slaughtering yard.

A man kicks her in the head
on her way past him,
dignity and grace
still in her eyes.

The Cook

What is this chef, this cook
that comes to gather
strung out, grumbling
friends and relatives?

Is she not a mere merchant
of the kitchen?
An employee of a restaurant?

But no, I think:
a magician or alchemist,
one who binds up the disgruntled
by cooking magic.

Her creations stir in
the hearts of these people
a language of love
they have never felt before,
or ever will.

Why, these two are speaking
when they haven't for years!

I think it must have been
that rare French wine, or,
perhaps that unusual, roasted
animal from the forest.

The Lake

In the cold winters
around the Great Lakes,
ice moves
in constant, fluid motion,
making cracking sounds,
thundering sounds,
as ice heaves against ice,
shelf against shelf,
sending echoes out
across a cold, stiff night,
that sound like a war
being waged,

like someone shooting off cannons
in some distant place.

She is telling us:
she is still here;
she is still alive!

Whiteness

On earth
there are no elements
of humankind
that work in harmony,

but in the whiteness
of snow there are.
The whiteness is like
no other white.

The snowshoe rabbit
this morning looked
brown against it.

White is holy.
It fights back
the grayness
that is human

and wins —
for a few moments.

Threads

The threads
on the hem of the skirt
have been pulled out,
leaving the earth
jagged and uneven,
wounded
like the trapper
this morning
ripping the fox
from the trap
after crushing its skull,
leaving the lake's edge
uneven.

Threads pulled out.

Threads
that bound us
that morning
as a gray fox
sprang in front of us,
a delightful look on his face,
as he carried his prey in his mouth.

Unearthly

Stillness,
except for the sound of water
running in rivulets
down the face of cliffs
to the Great lake:
that is earthly.

Sandhill cranes
landing
as if on skirts of air,
suspended in mid-air,
slowly coming down
to start their spring dance:
unearthly.

The Visitation

They were both
hanging by threads,
trying to hold together,
exhausted,
talking to people:
lost yet another child.

But those threads
will widen,
grow strong
when they decide to live
again

for the living —

like the herd of deer at dusk
we saw when we drove
back across the white frozen fields
in a clearing
on the side of a steep hill,
clinging to threads
in a trampled field
surrounded by deep winter snows.

White Blossoms on a Branch

When all human
intervention has harmed us,
when all *familia*
have spent the fruits,
then the Great Spirit
gives to us our opening
from the darkness,

from the going down
into the pit of our own agony,

a candle,
a birth, a rite
into a new life.

Then we are assured —
like the mother tiger
who reassures her young
that they belong
to a family,
that they are important
in this world.

This is what it's like —
white blossoms on a branch.

Winter Solstice

She rolled
up the mat,
turned out
the lights,
and we were plunged
into darkness.

December is like
living in a cave,
but the earth
will not hear of it,

unfolds her fetal position
in her darkened room
and allows light to emerge
longer in the morning
and afternoon —

sunlight able
to warm our deepest bones.

An Angel of Sorts

To Ed DiMaio

I must tell you
that sometime
when all is lost,
when there is
no more hope in the world,

the great cosmos,
the lovely universe,
puts on our path
a free spirit,
an angel of sorts,
or a person of faith —

and says,

"Here is your protector,
the one who will lift your soul up,
the one who has come
this evening to be your guide
to position yourself again
in the universe."

And now he says,

"How comely you are,
how lovely your skin,
how grand your soul."

Now you have your answer,
the answer to hopelessness:
unexpected grace.

Blue Above Us, Blue Below Us

We stepped off
the edge of the world today,
blue above us,
blue below us,

nothing but sky and water
around us
until
death's door
surprised us.

Not yet.
Not yet.
This is still not
yet our time.

Captured Memory

We are going
to a movie
in Minneapolis.
He spoke.

Brokeback Mountain
is showing,
he grinned.

A willing mother,
surrounded by a sea
of young men,

a twinkling
in his eye —

a captured memory
in a wind of thoughts.

End

His breathing
became ragged.

It was a rainy day.

At 6:00 p.m.
he passed away.

I was with him,
finally alone,
all afternoon.
I told him I was sorry
he had to endure
this ending.

A woman doctor
came up from
a different floor
to say to me
that when we die,
we choose the people
we want to be with.

It's Been Too Long
Since We Last Talked

It's been too long
since we last talked.
I must tell you
that men have had
their way with her.

She is hurt and sick,
but keeps giving us gifts,
ignoring their torture
and disrespect.

Today she surprises us
with the white hares.
They hop over each other,
making giggling sounds,
laughing at the prairie grasses.

She gives the spring rain
that coaxes green buds.
Soon we will plant
tomato and egg plants.

She gives us seeds to sprout,
not darkness, nor pain,
nor death.

Unheard Prayer in the Ancient Ruins

Let me tell you
that the old gods
will not help us.

When we pray
by the wayside
they will not
listen to our tears.

For they are deaf,
stone deaf

like the ancient boulders
we walked between
this morning —
cold and unconcerned —
among the sweetness
of blooming honeysuckle.

How Hard

We talked about children,
their schooling,
their boyfriends,
how they are becoming
serious about their relationships.

We talked about children
becoming people,
how hard it is.

We talked about
how hard creating
a new piece of art is,
how much energy
the making of art takes —
an extraordinary piece of art.

How hard that is:
like the yellow orchid
in the forest this morning
among the blue waters;
how hard the earth struggled
to bring about that flower:

like my ancestors
that were sailors,
sailing to other lands —
among the blue waters —

how hard.

The Reader

He has taken
his dinner with delight,
relishing each morsel,
tasting each bite
by rolling them
on his tongue.

He mouths the words,
forming them
on his lips,
smiling,

as he escapes
to his world —
the one called ecstasy.

Power

The sailor
understands
the power of the wind,

adjusts his sails
to capture it.

Sound of Breathing

This morning
the wind through the trees
sounded like air
through giant bellows,

like large lungs
breathing in air
and out air,

like we felt,
next to our mother
as infants,
a great pair of lungs
that we knew somehow was

the source of life.

Respite

We walked Michigan's shore
against gale winds,
blue-green water
churning up white foam
and throwing large rocks
at our feet

until a stand of cedars
offered warmth and stillness
from the wind.
Leaf-litter
lined the forest floor, softness,
respite from our difficult world.

Homestead

You said the house
was gone.
I said it should be leveled.
It wasn't a good house.
It was part of
an old train station
with additions put on.

But you meant
the family was gone,
didn't you?

The warmth of those
six people was gone,
the closeness, or
not such closeness,
was gone:

the mother carrying
lunch in a pail
out to the field
so the workers
could finish haying,

the long summer days
and snow filled winters
that surrounded that house
were gone.

That's what you meant, wasn't it?

People

There have been
periods of time
in history
where the people
have had power,

periods of peace
where rulers
have been peaceful,
and people have had
their say.

But now,
we, as people,
have lost our power.
We are living
in a period
of war and injustice:

like the ancient civilizations
where despots ruled
with reigns of terror
for millennia.

Jingle Bells

In winter
sleigh bells went around
the bellies of the black and bay,
four velvet ears ahead of us,
jingle bells on black harnesses.

It was in deep snow
when all was quiet,
and the horses began to trot,
that magic began to happen,

when eurythematic music
of a prancing, running march
through forested land
filled the air,

prancing feet
touching down into our hearts.

Chokecherries

Ripe chokecherries
on the branch
remind me
of the bitterness
of winter's coming.

Goddess

The hem of her dress
brushes against the trees
and the open meadows,
open spaces that bank
against the forest,
appearing familiar,
as if they were
from some other lifetime:

brushing that brings
into focus
the sharpness
of the fox's eyes
and the grass snake
that climbed
up into the cedar tree
to escape the flooded ground.

She is eye-level to us,
holding her head high,
looking into us
and we into her.

Escape

Canadian geese,
gleaning after
the harvesting tractor,
are like
the soul searching
for a place
to enter,
or escape,
into the shafts of light —
like the light
outside the basement door
this morning …

Or was it two maples
that propelled me
across the bay?

Or the wing
of the Monarch
in the afternoon's late light?

I Dream of A Different World

I dream of
a different world:

one where I can
take refuge,[1]

where you and I
will be sisters,

where the First Peoples
are striding along
with the Second peoples,
learning from each other,

where they are no longer refugees
in their own land,

where the freed slaves·
are helped to build
new lives with the colonists,
no longer refugees
in this new land.

I dream of
a different world,

where no one is heard
shouting from a window,

"Go back to where you came from."

---

[1] The first two stanzas are a quote from Ariel Dorfman, a refugee.

Holding My Breath

I keep looking
for the breathing holes
beneath this thick sea ice,

a place where
I can propel
up towards the light,
grasping for a breath of air
that smells like earth
and soil and green things.

I keep looking
for that rare space
because I cannot hold
my breath much longer.

There. Over there
I see some light
through honey-colored ice.

An Evening

For Sophia and Phoebe

Because this night is filled
with black-winged pelicans
coming in to land,
a sail being taken down,
a sliver of a moon
climbing above
the white birch trees,
and laughter from young girls
rising above the lapping waves,
no more can fit
into the evening.

A Day

It is a day
when the earth
turns just right,
when fish swim
close to the top
of the Great Lake
to feed on insects or plants,
when black-winged pelicans
dive in and out to fish,
and fishermen gather
in clumps, throwing
out their lines.
It is a day
before the storm,
humid and cloudy,
when the two of you
think of ways to
come together
as part
of a turning of the universe,
a love that blows
a sweetness over us —
something unexpected.

Biographical Note

Ethel Mortenson Davis is a poet and artist who lives in Sturgeon Bay, Wisconsin. She studied art at the University of Wisconsin — Madison and has had her poetry and art published in international anthologies, magazines, and literary journals. Her art has been featured in galleries in New Mexico and Wisconsin.

Her first book of poetry, *I Sleep Between the Moons of New Mexico*, was published in 2010 when she and her husband, the poet and novelist Thomas Davis, lived in Continental Divide, NM. It contained poems "as condensed and glittering as the facets of a diamond" as it explored the New Mexican landscape and its diverse people.

In 2011 her first book was quickly followed up by *White Ermine Across Her Shoulders*. More personal in tone, but still containing imagistic poems about nature, it contained a number of poems about the death of her son Kevin Davis.

In 2016 she published a small chapbook called *The Healer*. By this time she had moved to Sturgeon Bay, Wisconsin to be close to her two daughters, Sonja Bingen and Mary Wood, and her four grandchildren, Sophia and Phoebe Wood and Will and Joey Bingen. The poems explore the healing process and sometimes sing off the page with powerful, wonderful, or searing images.

Then, later in 2016, she published *Here, We Breathe In and Out Sky, Poems of New Mexico*. These were the last poems written during her years as a member of the Zuni Mountain Poets.

Made in the USA
Monee, IL
30 September 2021